when they come

MORGAN CHRISTIE

Published by Black Sunflowers Poetry Press
www.blacksunflowerspoetry.com

ISBN: 978-1-8382516-1-1

TABLE OF CONTENTS

INTRO NOTE

Black Sunflowers called out and from across the globe, poets answered. The cries of being and feeling were strange, funny, primal, otherworldly, and angry. Poems raged and fluttered, moaned, and muttered, soared and stumbled. From all the speakings, this voice was heard.

Enjoy,

Geffen Bankir
Amanda Holiday

"and what if colonization could be a satirical sci-fi epic"

— some imagined ghost

in the end

—

the goldfish will go first
attempting to digest their own fins

murder in the first
they'll call it

and all the remaining goldfish
will end up in goldfish prison

where they'll be force fed the remains
of their dead brethren

the prison will be run by marigolds
they stopped pretending after we left

they were of stature once
regal muchness and strong strides

but they were hunted for it
slaughtered in droves

so they became still
swallow   the odd pluck

for in comparison,
there was no comparison

the other domestics will go next
dogs standing the best chance

maybe not before the ones in captivity
can you imagine a zoo?
droves of wild
starved behind steel or

glass reflecting who they were
and who they are

but not before the goldfish
the goldfish will go first

——

and our girth will smell of dried and soiled orange peels

lemon heads and pond scum stuck between a pterodactyl's
connective tendons
          hovering under seary skin

its wings pushed under themselves out of fear of taking flight
with nowhere to go
                    but a gust will come and lift those
brilliant bones from their nest and drop the beast into the sky

sparrows will stare at the tumbling carcass
onyx wings tucked at their sides
          sugar ridden, fumed flickered and fallen

the flying bones would plummet into a toucan
right slam into its big yellowish bill   night wings
                              rouge ripples

the toucan would fall faster than the bones that left it for
dead
and the sparrows wouldn't be so sure it was an accident

the earth would spread and the carcass tremble
but before the bones shattered into pieces upon
pieces scattered around that fat lifeless toucan

               the pterodactyl will glace out among the
     growing trees

                    and picture itself sewing the skies
it will hear peace, the kind it knew before us
and want to hum its part
                    even though it's part
                    didn't exist

—

when the magic's gone
            folding over the cosmos
            and mapping the coup

cross fires with long strokes
of grey-teal and pops of purple
            fish that swim above
            water because bubbles
are so last year

corpses raised and werewolves
will finally crawl the moon
            their howls became
            divisive not long
            after we left
some evolved motor springing from
their vocbrations that propelled
            the beasts towards the
            things they howled at

they'd land in tall oaks
from time to time
            or atop the remnants
            of those scrapes in the
            sky bleeding the clouds

            the irony
earth was finally theirs

        its peaky graves
        warmed bergs
        hollow hills
        indented edges
        bitter cane

theirs for the taking and
they were confined to the moon
            unable to howl down at the
            place they most wanted to be

——

they took the menials   instantly
homes, clothes, toys, toothbrushes
and combs
we missed the combs
more than we expected to
our roots twisted and snarled
like a tiger might
not one in captivity
because we relied on those menials

and they needed us to rely on them

vanity is funny this way   yes
to make a thing beautiful
we o so complained about our hair
that we at least had the right to comb our hair
curly, straight, thick, thin, long, short
we just wanted the combs back
like a bird might
want to keep their feathers
because we relied on still feeling this way

but they needed us to rely on them

so they decided to fix it   then

to make it easier for us to cope
they shaved us all everywhere and it was gone
the hair, inches and miles of bare dry skin, gone
they took it all
not just the stuff on our heads
like a person might
for too many reasons to count
because we relied on our ability to choose

and now we needed to rely on them

—

just before we've climaxed, materialized
into some half formed thing
            the bodied hum of an offspring
we will glance across the way
on the hollow barrels they mounted us in
stacked together
toes to heads shoulders to elbows
reminiscent
            yes
and we'll be lifted from the world we knew
where we walked and detested and

we will glance across the way
into the only things left resembling us

whites of our eyes not so white
yellows of our teeth not so yellow
browns of our ducts not so brown
reds of our vessels not so red
blacks of our pupils not so black

what's left will look upon the rest
hearts dilated pupils beaten and
for the first time we'll finally see

each other, somewhere after the finish line
—

it's always
        the children

emptyheaded automatons
mouths rinsed in regurgitation

but they are the future
so it's always
        the children

they came for them
not ours
them

those soon planted seeds
dropped in red soil
a runnier red than they imagined

their offspring wouldn't spring
something about their pods

so they needed more
warm vessels to carry their lives

because what's a race that ceases to exist

they needed
bodies
just bodies
live bodies

they'd pollinate our plasma
we'd wash it down with a side of bile
and in a year we'd be them
the spiny backed giants with thin legs and arms

and we wouldn't remember anything of this life
and so many tasted grief
others ingested joy

those who resisted
were forced not to

how do you stop the unrelenting

but those that could threw themselves
into oceans, until they were plucked out
others off cliffs but were caught
at the bottom
and some resorted to the ground
pounding skulls into its crevasses
but they made the ground soft

they didn't want us hurt
            they wanted the children
not ours
them
salvation

            they said it a symbiosis
so it was completely natural

what does it mean to depend on

once changed
our bellies would carry
            the women's?
everyone's

our stomach the barer of spawn
versus delicious oils and cheeses
our minds the teachers of -

                          we did not know

they had been
          they
          for so long
we never thought to ask

their names

and when we did
they said it didn't matter
          they were only here
for the children

in the middle

—

two new religions germinated
as did several hymns that most hated
the songs just didn't measure
what would against a treasure
besides, aren't most hymns overrated

of course they are, and extremely dated
could have made it better if we waited
like that ballad *pressure*
we hard, by jah cure
but we settled for silver plated

maybe we're just poorly fated
as in the way those of troy were baited
we should have made it pure
to emulate their grandeur
just a bit better associated

they were the 'it' thing which translated
to the fashionable gods which created
that bold new show 'endure'
where you had to fly and your
lone condition: be uncalculated

the costumes bright, finely decorated
and the show's g-rating mandated
then once, for viewer allure
they guest starred, rating saviors
for who did not watch the awaited

their faces everywhere, us fixated
they did a coke add, we celebrated
they embraced our praise and we were elated
—

they spoke our languages, all of them
years of listening will do that
oprah got the exclusive
ten of their most handsome went to harpo

they took forever in makeup
something about the shade of their scales

and went onto a patio where they were
offered tea and salami and cucumber

what *do* you eat?
they never said

she asked them in that way she does
why earth, why now?

it will be the first time we see their teeth
or fangs or pincers or needles

and they'll look as though it was the thing
they'd been waiting for us to ask

we are with you and will rescue you

they'd passed millions of worlds
but none like ours

they didn't understand
they didn't understand us

they saw the love though
in spurts too notable

so they waited a millennia to be sure
for us to prove them right

we did
they chose earth because they wanted to
make us better

they chose earth
because someone needed to
and they told us not to worry

we'd find out what they ate
when we got there

—

people of earth…
we will make this brief
for our intent is simply to inform
the time has come

because we have decided to make this brief
we will remain blunt and immovable
the time has come
for our departure from your world

we will remain blunt and immovable
as we know what is best for you
so in our departure from your world
you will join us

we know what is best for you
and our need supersedes your own
you will join us
and you will know what it means to thrive

our needs supersede your own
but we are not monsters
you will thrive
and together we will be

we are not monsters
just beings as you are
and together we will be
greater than you have proven you could

we are just beings as you are
we will help you become
greater than you have proven you could be
because we have been watching

we will help you become
like the egyptians and greeks
because we have been watching
the way you idolized them

the egyptians and greeks
those gods they worshiped and adored
oh how you idolized them
how you have idolized us

those gods that were adored and worshiped
they fed on your love and desires
you need not idolize us
you will become all that we are

we will not feed on your love or desire
but we also do not require your understanding
you will be all that we are
do not worry, we know what is best for you

we do not require your understanding
only your compliance
we know what is best for you
and the process will begin shortly
your compliance
will be had
the process will begin shortly

people of earth…

you will be had
shortly
people of earth…
take heed

——

the problem was this had happened before

the crisis will make the eight o'clock news
and the world will be in a panic, not a wild
panic, more like a tempered frenzy that
evoked control and disarray all at the same
time, any station not covering their
announcement shifted to badumbadumeaking
news, reports were coming in on channels
one, two, three, four, five, six, seven, eight
you get it – we were in yielding hysteria
because even though we knew our cries
pointless our tears still needed a place to go

the problem was this had happened before

they watched as droves of us circled
their ships and others ran as far as their
short legs could take them, those runners
picturing them sucking our beer and
buttered bones if and after we set that
resistance back in place, but how could
we resist now if we couldn't resist then,
at least then we did not know what they
wanted from us, but, we still didn't know

the problem was this had happened before
and they knew it had, because they were the
stars and had been watching and waiting,

and now they were here, and they had seen
all the times before, where worlds were
built and broken the same way because
someone has to benefit and someone has
to lose and we don't much care about how
the losers feel about having become losers,
and the repercussions, what repercussions,
those only existed for the losers, but we
wouldn't be losers because they were
doing it for our benefit, and the truth was
that we were their teachers, and everything
that they had learned to do, everything they
had learned to take, they had learned from us

the problem was, this had happened before

in the beginning

—

the moon will howl
strips of orange and warning first
the sounds morph to tongue
and scratch against shadow

they'll come in
droves of metallic crystal
reflecting their light onto her
like she is some small thing

her howl will
bleed then and she'll hope the
roaches have not taken to
ears and feathered fuchsia to eyes

that we'll hear
the unified hush and blistered
milieu that looms from the stars
and climbs the strands of world

she'll wince
choke on her craters when she
sees that way of milk contort
into parallel pieces

they are the stars
and have been watching
and have been waiting
and have been here

she'll howl louder
watch as they grow and hope that
it's supple - stout enough to reach
down and dig dirt deep

so the roaches run
as the feathers hide and the rest
strain their lobes to listen for the
stars they do not hear coming

———

transcripts came from the water
        off the coast of osaka
pacific salt riding the encode's tail
the message blipped
        ..hiyato..
                ..hiyato..
and militaries escaped their
bunkers to see if it true
        ..confirm..
their schemes gusted
like a basiliscus to water
        silently no doubt
        ..confirmed..
they'd have to work together
and when the time came
the word would be
        ..hiyato..
                ..hiyato..
as it was in the beginning
        some saw them in the east
others in the north west
south
they were all around
        they were the stars
no one could detect what
their ships were made of
        and all attempts at
communication ignored

they were getting closer
        they needed to be stopped
governments bared arms
united together in preparation
        their citizens
                        us
        still in ignorant bliss
but the world leaders came
together
and waited by their
phones radios and computers for
        ..hiyato..
                ..hiyato..
and a general sat on the japanese
coast
counting down
--go--
        as the world waited
for the word that would
change everything
        --shi--
a word that wasn't just a
        word
to the general
                --san--
but the last thing
his son heard
as he neared that cliff
                        --ni--
some fifty feet high
        and as his baby feet
slipped from the earth
                        --ichi--
then the general called out
        as he did on that day
into a mic for all the world to hear
        ..hiyato..

                    ..hiyato..
and the switches were flicked
          buttons pressed
          levers pulled
so the bombs flew
nukes away
          hydrogen and atomic alike
blasted the ships with everything
in the arsenal
and the rest of us heard but
          very few paid attention
when the sky set a blaze
in glorious devastation
          and when the fire cleared
they continued for earth
unscathed as they were before
          so many floored and still
they watched as the general did
all those years ago
          at another type of downfall
          ..hiyato..
                    ..hiyato?..

——

imagine   the extra boy peering from some near distance
rooftop
or that we all still read enough for him to accrue a retirement
package

he   thought, "i'll shout 'extra extra read all about
it – stars turn to spaceships'
and people will swear i mean the ones in hollywood and think
it a new trend"

and   he'd be daring, anyway, hurdling from rooftop
to rooftop
because he'd always been an athletic boy with a knack for
leaps and bounds

his   mission, as he'd chosen to accept it, was to
find an epicenter,
a place we would all be and he could be the first to spread the
news

papers   flew from his bag as he jumped rooftops and
headed for the
place he was sure we were, and he wasn't wrong, we were

still   he knew it would take some time to get our
attention
when was the last time we paid the paper boy any mind

meant   he would do it though, so he shouted and
screamed cries of
papery despair, but no one looked up, but the birds fluttered a
bit

something   clicked then, as if the illustrious light bulb lite
itself and nearly imploded
he threw every paper down from the rooftop and watched it
rain his warning

               we only took out our umbrellas

——

they touched down like peddles to water
or crumbling bells but gently
a kiss, and the ground rippled beneath us

as a swatch would that hadn't been cared for
angry that it hadn't known its own glory
even though we did not all see them

we all felt them
dark glossy like onyx submerged in water
their ships, a measure of their glory
dominating the earth so gently
as millions of them landed in unison for
reasons that completely evaded us

but they were here, they and us
only we and them
they spoke to the world, 'we come in peace for
we wish you no harm, our vessels like water
absorb power you see', they explained gently
our defenses now a speck of their former glory

now, theirs was the only glory
perfection, they went on 'it is just us,
we do not wish you harm, just to gently
open our doors and step out of them
like an anxious fish out of water'
it was what we'd all been waiting for

no, what we'd all been yearning for
if they and their carriers were of similar glory
we'd have to start a resistance, as oil to water
what other choice did we have, it was up to us
because they came and we couldn't kill them
and then they opened their ship doors, gently

and the thought of a resistance fled as gently
as it came, their cryptic splendor too potent for
most, we couldn't take our eyes off of them
their color, so deep it almost black, green glory
rounded spiny backs, all giants, nothing like us
thin, long legs and arms we wanted to dip into water

because to dip a thing into water
means it knows how it feels to be pulled out of it, like us
what if they knew how to feel, in all their splendid glory
—

we
tempered, rancorous
questioning, questioning, (did i mention) questioning
dubious but distinctly drawn
(the) people

we
reflecting, mirrored
pools of angst
milieus of worried wheat bending in anything but wheat
fields
(those) people

we
complacent, (both ways)
too frightened to understand the ones that understood it all
too proud to try not to be frightened
(these) people

—

not long after they came
they started to fly
without their ships
swarming above us in droves
waving politely as we waved back
the giants and the small things
they didn't even have wings
so it seemed more a
levitation than flight really
and their tongues were

thick and sandy like a cat's
we heard them gruel, not growl
once, it seemed the way they
communicated but it didn't
scare us, it seemed a thing
we'd been hearing forever

their wonder caused mirrors to
shatter as vanity had yet
to meet a thing like them
and they laughed at the mirror's
narcissism as the shards cut their
soles before they whisked away

then the only day i foresaw
came to light, when a people
would walk outside and parallel the
streets, long lines stretching around
the world, hands up and palms out
in front, arms wide and legs lengthen as oak timber before the
fall
they'll be flailing, our hands,
whining to the sky, our deep embered skin in
droves lined up reaching upwards
whispering songs of rejoice and
flare, as the other dark bodies smile
down at the ones of us whistling up

take us, take us with you
...what do we have to lose
...what do we have to lose!
...what do we have to lose?
...what do we have to lose.

"then maybe..."

Black Sunflowers Poetry Press

Backed by an array of artists, activists, poets and poetry fans from all walks of life, Black Sunflowers, the UK's first crowdfunded poetry press, came into being in March 2020 with a pledge to publish and promote the work of women, older women and black poets from the UK and around the world. Black Sunflowers is grateful to Nat West's #BackHerBusiness scheme, all the supporters including Patrick Bill, Amanda Sebestyen, Cathy Greenhalgh, Rehana Zaman, Rob Curry, Nadine Marsh-Edwards, Rosa Fong, Judah Attille, Elinor Perry-Smith, Monika Baker, David Curtis, Oona Hyland, Janice Cheddie, Simone Alexander, Mustapha Feika, Michael Cadette and others who wish to remain anonymous, as well as the additional enterprise finance awarded to us. Black Sunflowers is thankful to those who have offered encouragement and advice along the way and who have contributed their skills or inspired through their own publishing entrepreneurship.

Embarking on this venture during Covid19, on the cusp of a lockdown was challenging and perhaps folly. Yet, with daily life on hold, this has been a time for deep reflection for all of us. A time perhaps to pause for poetry.

www.ingramcontent.com/pod-product-compliance
Lightning Source LLC
Chambersburg PA
CBHW032135050726

47590CB00008B/3112